WINCHESTER

A POETIC HISTORY IN INCONSEQUENTIAL MOMENTS

Created and edited by
Jonny Fluffypunk for
Winchester Poetry Festival

Acknowledgements

Winchester Poetry Festival is grateful to Winchester City Council, Winchester BID, the National Lottery Heritage Fund and individual donors for their support of the *Poet in the High Street* project.

We are also grateful to the many businesses and other organisations who helped with the project, hosting pop-up events and poetry stalls, telling their own stories and even providing the odd free pie to keep Jonny's strength up.

We are also, of course, indebted to the people of Winchester, without whom this book would be much shorter.

Credits

Contents

PART II: PEOPLE, PLACES & PROJECTS   93

AN INVOCATION

Poet on the High Street:
In the Footsteps of John Keats in Winchester

i.

The feets of Keats
walked these streets
back in the year of 1819;

He wrote his ode to Autumn here,
then threw in the towel with poetry
no more wrangling consonant and vowel
for John; time to move on to something better
paid.

But for those last few weeks
as servant of the muse
John's poetic fuse burned bright;
through stubble fields and city gates,
in the lowering light of September, he
found a profound grace;
he kept his eye to the sky
and his ear to the ground

the latter a matter
he found easy to do –
though John's stature in poetry grew enormous,
he stayed five foot two.

ii.

John found this town a pleasant one, if a little
dull;
he remarked about the need for a bit of
excitement.

The side streets too maiden-lady-like,
the door knockers too freshly gleamed;
the click of a walking cane is regarded as riot.
Winchester is, in John's own words, a bit *awful
quiet*.

#Blessed   *Steve Scholey*

St Swithun-upon-
Kingsgate, St Bartholomew's,
St Stephen's, St Faith's, St Cross,

St Michael's, St Martin's,
St Mary's and St Matthew's,
St Andrew's, St Barnabas,

St Luke's and St Laurence's,
St Peter's, St Paul's, St Thomas's,
St James, St Giles, St John the Baptist –
so many holy houses, we are surely
#Blessed.

PART I: THE MAP OF UNFORGETTABLE MOMENTS

About This Book and How to Use It

This isn't a 'proper' poetry book, in the traditional sense, but then there's plenty of those around, and some of them are brilliant. Neither is it a 'proper' guidebook; I mean, you won't learn much of the *official* history of Winchester here, but again, there's plenty of *proper* guidebooks around.

So what is it? Well, it's part poetry, part documentation of an arts residency, and part an arty-farty symbolic remapping of a city. A Poetic Handbook for a Pilgrimage With No Destination.

We are more than just spectators in someone else's city.

We are not incidental to the place we live. On the contrary, all of us are active agents in this many-layered, ever-unfolding story called Winchester; our many thousands of parallel narratives are each vital cells in the body of a living, breathing beast. The genius loci; the Spirit of Place.

Winchester, we are reminded from a thousand websites, brochures and guest-house noticeboards, is *HISTORY,* with a capital everything. It is a place of ancient cathedrals, prominent bishops, hallowed schools, and long-dead kings. There are brown roadsigns, blue plaques and (I've checked) whole ranges of souvenir tea-towels. How are we little humans – in the here and now, with our petty comings and goings, hopes and fears, our silly little everyday life-battles – how are we supposed to compete with that? We're not; were supposed to just fit in around it as best we can.

Keep Calm and Carry On Shopping

In any large conurbation, but especially somewhere like this, that fancies itself as a 'destination attraction', authorities work very hard to promote the 'brand', and employ all manner of tactics to shape and funnel our experiences, energies and desires in ways beneficial to their (usually commercial) intentions. You'll notice this on the 'artist's impressions' that accompany the promotion for new developments – shopping centres, housing complexes, and the like. All those fashionably-clothed stick people, happily browsing the avenues of shops, sitting at the pavement cafes, admiring the generously-provided minimalist fountains. There's never anyone shagging in the bushes, passed out on the benches, or spray-painting the walls.

Yet, as this book, in part, gloriously celebrates, our collective humanity continues to triumph over the narrowed outlooks imposed on it. In the poems and fragments gathered here are multiple instances of irrepressible humans gleefully giving the finger to all the *KEEP OFF THE GRASS* signs and redefining their relationship with their environment on their own terms: using an alleyway as a boudoir, consecrated ground as a boxing ring, public space as an assault course. Or bar.

Or toilet.

These tiny subversions of public space are things to be celebrated; they prove that beneath the dignified image, real Winchester is alive and kicking. But by no means everything recorded here is 'naughty'; far from it. Many of the moments people generously shared with me in the course of this residency are gloriously mundane. Everyday meet-ups, break-ups and cock-ups. Sites of toddler tantrums and places where someone has just sat silently and breathed. But *all* of these inconsequential moments from anonymous lives are to be celebrated, not just the cheeky ones; all of them are tiny poetic X's marking spots where, once, in a moment of time, LIFE happened.

So, although I artily suggested this book is a handbook for 'a pilgrimage with no destination', perhaps what this pilgrimage is really about is carving out a break in our busy schedules to just honour *life – that* wonderful, relentless miracle; that impossible magic that it so ubiquitous it just flies by, unnoticed.

So, let's notice it. Forget about cathedrals, and bishops, and King bloody Alfred. Let's notice ourselves. Notice each other. This book is an encouragement to raise a glass to our little triumphs, our micro-failures. *We* built this city, after all... on rock 'n' roll, yes – played on a crappy cassette on the steps of the Buttercross – but also on fish 'n' chips, artisan coffee and kisses in the park.

Let's all become Counter-Tourists.

Now, that's not my idea – I'm indebted to the work of arts activist, theatremaker, and cultural guerrilla Phil 'Crab Man' Smith, who coined this concept as part of a strategy to reclaim our history, heritage and sense of self back from those who would prefer to sell us a particular version of it. Note it's *counter*-tourist, not *anti*-tourist; strip away the bad press and connotations, and tourists are, as Smith asserts, a sort of pilgrim: *'the beach or monument their shrine; self-transcendence (bodies tanned, minds broadened) their Grail'*. Human beings out to transform themselves through experience. It's just that there's a multi-million pound industry working to influence what form that experience should take.

As Counter-Tourist, with this book as a guide, I encourage you to choose to approach the places and the moments detailed in the poems, apercus and haikus in this book in the same way one would an 'official' heritage site. Look at your city in a different way, and have *fun* doing it:

- Having read all about the moment, allow yourself to become excited as you approach the actual place it actually happened! What will it *look* like? What will it *feel* like?

- Wander around the spot, trying to put yourself in the shoes of the protagonist(s)

- Imagine the exact words said. Role-play the moment with friends!

- Sit on the fateful bench; stand under the exact tree; see the view *they* would have seen.

- Stop passers-by and get them to take your photograph at this historic spot.

- Pre-record the words before setting out, then listen back to them on headphones whilst nodding, pointing and staring.

- Think about some of the ritualistic behaviour that has developed at certain historic sites – kissing the Blarney stone, for instance, or sending rude words echoing round the Whispering Gallery – and come up with rituals for some of these places: spilling a votive offering of white cider over the Buttercross, perhaps, or re-creating wearing a brass divers helmet whilst jabbing at a phone and wailing outside the *William Walker*.

- Find your own ways to honour these fragments of ordinary lives; accord them the beauty they deserve.

Treat this book as a call-to-arms.

Every reader could, and should, create their own version of this book. We're all simultaneously tremendously important and utterly insignificant, and we're all part of where we live. So *go on*, celebrate yourself for a day! Take a map and a notebook; drift around the city. Let your memories bubble back up from the pavements and ooze from the walls. Nothing is insignificant. Write it all down! Maybe try to shape the words a bit; don't be scared because you haven't done this before. Find out that your life is at least 95% poetry! Perhaps make some of your scribbles into short little 17-syllable haikus. Perhaps develop others a bit more. Others still, just leave as fragmented thoughts. Perhaps it helps to view the slightest incident as an epic adventure with *you* as the hero? Go for it; write it down like that, tongue-in-cheek. There's no rulebook here; it doesn't have to be serious. It certainly doesn't have to be perfect.

You hold in your hands a challenge to remap Winchester; to boldly reshape it in your own image, to vision it through the kaleidoscope lens of glorious, technicolour subjectivity. Together we can pull all the overlooked doorways, neglected pavements and graffiti'd municipal seating out of the shadows and into the spotlight, where they belong. For these are the places *our* history, *our* heritage is made.

And, if we need a figurehead for this quest? Well, when I asked people to name a public figure they associated with the city, someone they held dear to their hearts, someone who should be honoured in monument and story and verse, one name came out a clear winner. So, come the glorious day when blue plaques mark street corners where we fell in love, and brown road signs point to the sites of our drunken collapses, perhaps then we shall see, atop a plinth at the foot of the High Street, carved in granite, not a distant king but instead, bold and bearded, pram at his side, Winchester's *real* favourite son.

Burping Ron.

Burping Ron

Someone said he had a flat
somewhere up on Fivefields Road
So, maybe not a full-on tramp
but he looked the part,
all beard and minging vest
and a trolley stuffed with
seven shades of shite –
cabbages, bottles, cans –

and you have to understand
the sun shone out behind the grime
a smile, a gift, a *never mind,
it'll soon be Christmas*
and, of course, his USP
was belching – full and free and
straight in people's faces.

A city needs its folks like this,
to stop it disappearing up its own backside.
Cadging fags outside the Mash Tun,
putting fear into the tourist hordes.

More than one said *the best thing
was, he made the place look untidy...*

The following text accompanied the laminated printed map of the city that I carried with me at all times during the Poet on the High Street residency; 'popping up' in the street, and in shops, cafes, bars and at events across Winchester, asking people to share moments, however banal, from their lives in the city. Some took the time to write haikus or other short poems, some just shared their stories and I noted them down as best I could, and shaped them into poems later. These pieces, plus pieces written by workshop participants, form the body of this book.

POET ON THE HIGH STREET 2021
THE MAP OF UNFORGETTABLE MOMENTS

Winchester is a city with a lot of heritage. Yes, we know the names of kings; we know where the bishops lived and where the big battles were fought.

But what about US? *We're* all fighting our own battles; *we* all live and love and hurt and grow. Places in this city etch themselves on our hearts and memories for our own special reasons. Kings and bishops are rarely involved.

This map aims to be a record of the beautiful and painful and unsung personal happenings that occur around us all the time, un-noticed and uncelebrated, amongst these streets and buildings and parks we know so well. This map marks our joys, our heartbreaks and our epiphanies; our tearful farewells, our drunken promises, our nights spent screaming at the stars.

Please take a moment to put yourself on the map.

It's colour-coded; mark as many of your moments as you like.

Let's get the underlying magic of the city to reveal itself!

The GENIUS LOCI! The SPIRIT OF WINCHESTER!

Perhaps certain street corners are FIRST KISS HOTSPOTS? Is a particular pub a DRUNKEN EPIPHANY NODE? Is there a STORM-OFF-IN-A-HUFF HUB beneath the sad gaze of that statue?

A HIDDEN HERITAGE OF EVERYDAY MARVELS!!!

SHARE YOUR STORIES!!

I need YOUR stories! As POET ON THE HIGH STREET, I am turning the findings of this map into poetry. Celebrating these places, and your moments! Turning everyday life into ART! I'd love it if you'd record one of your moments — however briefly, however anonymously — on one of the 'story slips' and pop it in the letterbox!

There will be POETRY BLUE PLAQUES for some of these places. And don't worry — any names will be changed. Your secrets will be safe.

LOVE & ROMANCE (inc. first kisses, instances of love-at-first-sight, first dates, proposals, conceptions, knee tremblers and other spontaneous romantic occurrences, etc)

EPIPHANIES (inc. life-changing realisations, sudden-dawnings, right-this-can't-go-on-a-moment-longers, get-yourself-togethers, etc)

MELANCHOLIA & DESPAIR PITS (inc. last farewells, break-ups, drowned sorrows, weeping drunkennesses, overwhelming regrets, utter nihilism, etc)

EUPHORIAS (inc. 'isn't-life-blimmin'-brilliant?-s, nights-to-remember, dancing-til-dawns, wildly happy drunkennesses, religious ecstacies, Ecstasy ecstasies, etc)

BOTHER ZONES (inc. tantrums, stormings-off, grief-off-strangers-s, you-want-some?-s, fisticuffs of all sorts, arrests, etc)

SUPERNATURAL (inc ghosts, UFOs, faerie folk, ball lightning, risings from the dead, etc)

OTHERS (what have I forgotten?)

Winchester: A Map of Unforgettable Moments

A self-guided walk through a subjective history of Winchester City, as told by its extraordinary inhabitants.

Most of these poems were written by Jonny, based on the stories and memories that people shared with him.

Where somebody's first name appears next to a poem, that person's story inspired the poem.

Where somebody's *full* name appears next to a poem, that person actually *wrote* the poem.

Map 1: St John's Church to Kingsgate

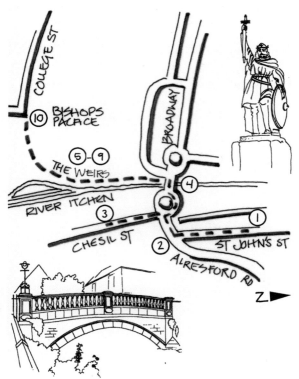

Start at St John's Church, St John's St, SO23 0HF

1. **St John's Church** *Jo Foster*

Pilgrims still pass this way:
Some bearing boxes marked 'Deliveroo'
Others on foot, weary, in high-vis
Or on scooters, the small ones hurtling
The bigger ones louche, with e-powered glide.
Here: one approaches, slouched and shifty on
his phone
He ducks into the churchyard
On the wall, a cockle shell
Notes him like the others: they all count.

*Turn right out of the churchyard into St John's St,
to the junction with Bridge St. The Rising Sun pub
is opposite.*

The Rising Sun

---

2. **The Hard Nut from Highcliffe**   *David H.*

is how we knew him, and he was.
Hardest man in all of Winch,
Fists like hams, and evil eye,
and all day in the Rising Sun.

All day on the cribbage board
sinking pints, moving pegs
building up to nightfall, when
unsteady legs would steer him
off, unerringly, to aggro.

And on the pub's dwarf-hurling days
I never saw a man hurl a dwarf
half as far as Perky Hayes.

And there, in a snapshot, is a measure
of the bloke: pissed-up, aggressive,
and completely un-woke.

*Walk down Bridge St toward the city centre; at the
mini-roundabout turn left onto Chesil St. Chesil
Theatre is just up on the right.*

3. Chesil Theatre   *Sam*

I landed my first 'Eating Parts';

stuffing my face with free bananas

in The Venetian Twins, then,

as Otter in Wind in the Willows,

stuffing my face with free sausage rolls,

clasped in my pauper actor hands

like flaky pastry Holy Grails.

*Retrace your steps to the mini roundabout and
turn left, over the ancient hump-back bridge. The
City Mill is on your right.*

4. **The Old Mill**   *Addy*

Well, we had a moment
in the tiny garden here;
a nothing moment. Nothing
happened, see. I just became aware
how green and full and lush, how full
of life it was. How beautiful.
The peace and quiet, how good it felt.
Is that enough? Should there be more...?

*Opposite the City Mill, go down the footpath
between the bridge and the pub. This path is
called The Weirs.*

Node Point #1: The Weirs

The next few poems take place along this path.

---

5. **A Bench along from The Bishop**   *Anon*

On Christmas Day,
on a bench beside the Itchen,
two lockdown lovers illegally meet.

There is moss. There is lichen.
There is mulled wine
warmed in the kitchen
of one of them, I'd guess.

And one of them pops a question.
And the other one says *yes*.

A bench on the Weirs

---

6. **The Melancholy of Sophia Loren**   *Anon*

I was sat on the bench
on the path to the water meadows
when a man stopped
and asked if I minded
if he took my photograph.
He explained
that a long time before
he had sat on this very bench
with the actress Sophia Loren.

It was 1974
and Sophia was in town
filming a remake of *Brief Encounter,*
a rehashing of the iconic that was
later to be slated as disastrous, pointless
and a miscasting bordering on lunacy.

The man said Sophia
had invited him, a passing stranger,
to sit, and she bought him a coffee
and talked for a bit of her troubles.
She was lonely, she said;

beauty and fame were lame substitutes
for being happy, being loved.

And it occurs to me
as we chat, that we are ourselves
sat remaking *his* Brief Encounter,
again badly miscast,
though we've no critics to witness,
no judgement to pass,
and ours seems more fun.

In the afternoon sun,
I think of Sophia sat here,
her glamour shot through
with sadness, suffused
with the blues, and this a full
year before she read the reviews.

---

7. **Bench on the Weirs**   *Catherine & Martin*

After 50 years and more of life,
and 30 years of marriage,

at last someone
has the grace to stop

and tell us
we look lovely.

8. **The Weirs Haiku** *Marian Kelly*

Christmas Eve kisses.
Never saw her after that,
but it was worth it.

9. **The Weirs Bike-u** *Jack L.*

I was so arseholed,
riding into the river
barely registered

*Follow the curve of the wall around to the right,
toward College St. The Bishop's Palace is on your
right as you reach the road.*

10. **Bishop's Palace Gardens** *Penny Monro*

Sprung carpet crocus
Bishop's lawn delights
Blois's shadowed spirit

*Carry on up College St. Winchester College is
behind the high wall on your left.*

Map 2: College St to Cathedral

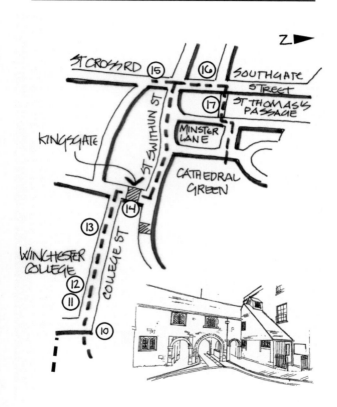

College Street

---

11. **Winchester College Carol Service**

Lynda O'Neill

The congregation appraises itself, discreetly.
I watch out for Wendy Cope,
    who's written the words for
a commissioned carol and just avoids
    being late.
You point out senior masters with
    policemen-young faces.

No incense this year, we note, and less coughing.
Pulpit lessons are read in confident
    Wykehamist tones
by suited, shirted boys, a look we'd like
    our own son to favour.
I have unsuitable thoughts about
    some of the older ones.

During the not always obscure tunes
I grieve for the sound I once made,
now feeble, low on acrobatics.

You drone, a foot and a semi-tone away,
aghast we're required to stumble through
O Come all ye Faithful in Latin.

I reflect on its sparseness at
 sixties secondary moderns.

But as its descant alerts my neck hairs,
I unwrap the memory of
 Mrs Zeffertt's quavering tones as
she taught it to us, and the years
 my young voice could have
touched the rafters of this lovely place,
gifting me a Christmas present forty years on.

---

12. **Outside Winchester College**   *Jo Foster*

My son mid-tantrum
Teenagers in suits come out
to stare, and say *Shame*.

*Carry on up College St, past the fake 'deathplace'
of Jane Austen (it's reckoned she REALLY died in a
now-demolished cottage on the right); P&G Wells
bookshop is on your left.*

13. **Fifteen Questions Regarding John Keats & Winchester's Oldest Bookshop**

Did John walk this way every day
or just once in a while?

Did he buy pens?
Did be buy books?
Did he buy a file
to keep his work in?

Was he an in-and-out bloke
or did he stay a while and lurk in
amongst the shelves?

Did John get his feet through the door
then follow with more of him?

Did John *buy* books
or just merely look,
and drink in the thinking
for free?

Did he hang around the counter?
Did he chat to the staff?
Was John a pain in the neck
or a bit of a laugh?
Did they know who he was?
How important he'd be?

Did they tip him a wink
and give him ink for free,
or at least at a good discount?

Did John ever treat himself
to a brand new pen?

And if he did, then when he left the shop
and returned to the streets
did they put a sign by those pens:
AS USED BY JOHN KEATS?

*Carry on up College St to the junction; the
Kingsgate arch is on your right, with St Swithun's
church straddling the gate. Go through the arch to
the church entrance. The lovely man from the
prints shop puts out chairs, so have a rest and a
chat.*

14. **St Swithun's Church** *Molly*

Inspired
by the little church
to bold and holy acts

my grand-daughter
turned to my friend and I –
just friends, and nothing more,
you understand?

I think you must get married, she said.

And so a little awkward, we were wed
in a child's makeshift ceremony.

Well go on, kiss each other then

and when we did
we were shocked to find
our awkwardness dissolved.

*Turn left as you come out of the Kingsgate arch,
with the door to St Swithun's church on your left.
Walk up St Swithun Street to the junction with
Southgate St / St Cross Road. Turn left for 200m to
the zebra crossing, just past St Michael's Rd. If
there's no traffic, stand in the road and pretend
you're in a car.*

15. **On St Cross Road** *Anon*

From nowhere, it seemed,
as if in a dream, first one, then two
then three hundred more
single-filed schoolboys
zebra-crossed before our
patient car.

To my eyes, it was
The Beatles *Abbey Road,*
if the Beatles were a smaller size
and if there was a load
more of them.

*Retrace your steps along St Cross Rd, heading
toward town. Just past the Everyman Cinema on
your left, stop at the corner of Archery Lane.
Pretend it's very late and the pubs are kicking out.*

16. **Archery Lane** *Mattanza*

It was the night of the fight;
Conor McGregor and
Floyd Mayweather Jr.

His fist a boxing glove of ignorance,
he slammed me up against a wall,
insisting Al Capone was an actor.

He called my fedora *a cowboy hat*,
then hurled it over an iron gate

It was the night of the fight:

Mayweather beat McGregor,
a knockout in the tenth.

Stupid Drunk beat Random Ectomorph,
a humiliation at half eleven.

*Continue along the road (now Southgate St)
toward town for another 20 metres. Turn right and
walk down a flight of steps into the alleyway
named St Thomas' Passage. There's a red phone
box on the corner. Try to picture it shrouded in
darkness; savour the mingled fear and excitement.*

17. **St Thomas' Passage** *Kai*

I remember you'd just finished your crisps,
scrunched the bag into the bin and then
we came down the steps and a few moments
later your salt and vinegar hands are under
my shirt and all over me; I can taste the
sharpness hanging on your mouth and you
are eating me and I am eating you, in a hot
insistent devouring moment, and if we are
watched, we are watched by invisible stars,
themselves devoured by the streetlights,
and we scared a cat who ran off
and got devoured by the shadows.

*At the bottom of St Thomas' Passage, turn left, and
then right onto Minster Lane. At the end of the
latter, turn left then immediately right and into
Cathedral Green, the open grounds in front of the
Cathedral.*

Map 3: Cathedral Area

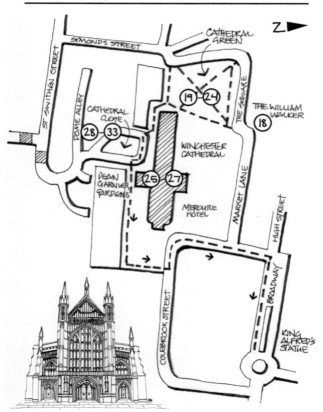

Node point #2: Cathedral

Cathedral Haiku

---

18. Cathedral Green: By The William Walker Pub

Mark

Jill phoned to end it.
No diver could shore up my
heart, stop it drowning.

---

19. Cathedral Flower Festival

Frank

An hour and a half.
If she makes me look at one
more sodding flower...

---

20. Royal Visit and a 3-year-old

Siobhan

The princess shakes young
Harry's hand; *I've one of these
at home*, she smiles.

21. **Cathedral Green, The Beech Tree**   *Kit*

We'd sit there, over by the wall
We like the shade see? Felt good
to grab those moments before
we'd get moved on

That tree, with all those roots
like it was flaunting it's belonging,
showing off how it could not be told
to shift, clear off, to sling it's hook

We had nothing, see?
I was crashing with Trish
on St Cross Road
and Marko had a trailer
tucked away down by the river

But this tree,
when I think about it
it kind of felt it understood
Nature doesn't care who you are
or who you aren't; this tree
made no judgement.

Sit on my roots, sit in my shade;
the leaves like so many
blind eyes turned.
No questions asked.

22. **Cathedral Green** *Matt*

Well, there was this time
we were walking back at midnight
and there was this guy
in the middle of the path,
dinner jacket, tie, the works,
and his trousers were round
his ankles and he was leaning
back and pissing in a great arc,
and he was singing, and the
thing was, I know it's gross,
but his voice was really loud
and clear and beautiful, it
echoed off the cathedral wall,
and he was bathed golden
by the streetlamps, and
in that moment, I felt
humanity really was
bloody magnificent.

That's probably
not the sort of thing
you're wanting,
is it?

23. **Cathedral Green in the company of 2nd Lt Andrew Chesterman #1** *Becks*

He guessed the way to this girl's heart,
he bought me a gorgeous pasty
And afterwards my lips met his
and I found them just as tasty.

24. **Cathedral Green in the company of 2nd Lt Andrew Chesterman #2**   *Becks*

On my way to the
Rifles Museum
to see his name

I came through here,
past the ghost
of our first kiss

I miss him
more than I can say

but today I can
sense him looking down
I can sense him everywhere

I can sense him in the dance of
a Greggs bag blown across the ground

I can sense him in the sound
of the starlings chattering above.

My soldier died in Helmand,
but not his love.

25. **Cathedral: The Crypt** *Lynda O'Neill*

My crypt's a long way from the Peckham studio
where Gormley birthed me. I like it down here,
apart from having wet feet most of the year.
Not as quiet as you'd think, though, away from
questing feet pounding the stones above,
mustering obediently around a tour guide.

School parties clutch clipboards,
    point and giggle at
my non-existent genitalia, unpeel a Mars Bar
before Sir's down the steps.

If it's Wednesday it must be the Americans,
baying, weighed down by camera tackle, their
Texas or Milwaukee accents chastened by
the seeping quiet.

The visitors I like best are alone.
They gaze at my featureless face,
forever tilted,

saying God knows what to
the unmoving water.

26. **Winchester Cathedral Gargoyle**

Sue Spiers

The chequer board of paths in Cathedral Green,
crossed cues on a baize snooker table
with black waste-bin pockets

People stroll in sea colours, ultramarine and
grey.
An occasional white sail of cotton blouse
drifts through that foaming ocean.

A ring of bells, a familiar opus in halting piano
lessons
from a college music room, distant buzzing
conversation from proxy statues.

Cappucino and croissant scent rising solemnly
from Pret's, Starbuck's and Costa's cafes;
blood and body of this century.

27. **Choir Practice in the Cathedral**

Caro Reeves

I met a fellow collecting verses
in the faceted city of Winchester
and he asked me which were my special places,
why had I been there, and when and where.

I thought of my times in that ancient city,
of the windy arches and shops and parks
where Bishops on bicycles
    dash round the corners
and the frocked and the defrocked
    bought knickers in Marks

I have trodden the footsteps of
    William of Wykeham
walked under the Kingsgate and
    round to the right
with several musical ladies and gentlemen
round about ten on a Saturday night.

Choir practice is not, as you
    might be supposing,
a placid event, like an unruffled stream,
with wonderful music, then home to a cocoa
with the man you once thought
    was the man of your dreams

Dear me no! You should know that
    romances can blossom
in the trembling hearts of Soprano and Bass,
In Tenor and Alto each buttoned up bosom
can crescendo and blend, oh,
    with such perfect grace

One Saturday evening, these feelings boiled over.
Two tenors squared up in the Close in the dark.
Growling like basses, the two would-be lovers
thrashed at each other with copies of Bach.

the watching sopranos had fits of hysteria,
the altos bunched bleating like terrified sheep
while the combatants fought 'neath the
    startled wisteria
til both of them fell in a furious heap.

After that little fracas,
    the blushing importunates
gave up the young lady and slipped off alone,
leaving others to tell all those
    eager unfortunates
who had missed the whole thing
    and gone quietly home.

*Exit Cathedral Green via stone archway to the
right of the cathedral, into Cathedral Close.*

Cathedral Close

28. **Christmas Fair, Cathedral.** *Chris*

It's not Christmas 'til it's there, I feel
The stalls glow the same yellow glow they had
was I was just eleven years old and the crowd
parted in the cold, exciting evening dark and
I glimpsed, between the jostling winter coats,
ice skaters, going round and round;
slow, graceful circumnavigations,
the way that seasons turn, or the world.

29. **1st Bench on R., Cathedral Close Haiku**
Martin

This was grandad's bench
We'd sit and talk. He'd bring crisps.
Monster Munch for me.

30. **Dean Garnier Gardens Haiku** *Liz & Sam*

The first love-selfie
we ever took together
here in Winchester.

31. **Courting Bench, Cathedral Close*** *Patricia*

That's where the courting couple sat
in 1948; it says so on the plaque
so when I saw this couple sat there,
hand in hand, I says *That's the courting
couples' bench! You must get married now!*
I understand how these things work, you see,
and love, it works like germs.

32. **Courting Bench Haiku** *Nathan Skene*

The poet named it
Courting Couples Bench;
It drew us back, under warm skies

*The Courting Bench can currently be found in
front of the Deanery. The benches are sometimes
shuffled around, so you might have to hunt for it.*

33. **Cathedral Close: The Deanery**   *Gill; Mark*

They built a wooden shack –*The Bit on the Side:*–
the origin of the term, I'm told –
    so Nell Gwynn's
ungodly form could be accommodated
    on this holy ground.
And Gill and 'unnamed other',
    Mark and 'unnamed other'
and doubtless hundreds more
    across the breadth of time
have, in the quiet shadows
    of this place, exchanged
a shifty kiss, a furtive grope
and more besides, I'd hope.

And all have prayed they went unseen
by the damning eyes of other halves,
never mind God.

Walk back toward the Cathedral. Exit Cathedral Close to the East, through arch and down pathway to Colebrook St. Turn left; follow Colebrook St round corner to the right.. Pause as you pass the Mercure Hotel on your left. Gaze up.

There were houses here once, and somewhere in the air, on what is now the first floor of modern hotel, John Keats sat staring at a blank wall, and wrote his ode To Autumn.

Shake your head, shrug, and walk out on to the High St.

Turn right, and head to the King Alfred statue, by the roundabout.

Map 4: High Street

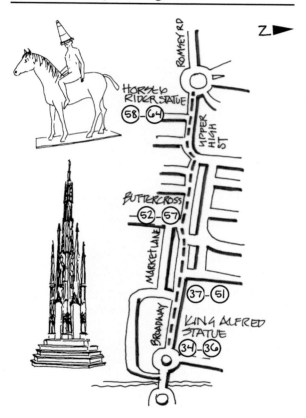

Z ▶

ROMSEY RD

HORSE & RIDER STATUE
58–64

UPPER HIGH ST

BUTTERCROSS
52–57

MARKET LANE

37–51

KING ALFRED STATUE
34–36

BROADWAY

Node Point #4: King Alfred's Statue

---

34. **King Alfred Statue:**
Football's Coming Home *Anon*

(A moment recorded during the 'days of hope'
that followed England's defeat of Denmark in the
semi-finals of the 2021 European Cup)

Football's coming home;
they were singing it from the bus
as I crossed the Broadway. It rose
from the garden of The Bishop on the Bridge –
Football's Coming Home, it's coming home.

And like a flag flown to herald its return,
someone's tied an England scarf around
the neck of old King Alf, sat up on his pedestal.

It's a thousand years since he himself saw off
the Danish threat; Gareth Southgate in a funny
iron hat. His jaw is set in cold, hard stone.

If he has any strategies for dealing with Italians,
he's keeping them to himself.

35. King Alfred's Statue:
The Keeper of Secrets   *Brenda Sedgwick*

It's Friday night and parents are
parked up, waiting.
My mouth is dry from yawning,
the car radio keeps me awake.

From Greens pub, a convoy of youth
reaches the Buttercross.
They walk on, past dimly lit shops,
heading for home before the bewitching hour.

Girls pull at their too short skirts,
the clipping of heels and giggles come closer.
Everyone shouts loudly their goodbyes
And boys swing on the bus stop.

Three girls identify my car.
Rings and false nails scrape at the door handles.
They jump in, sucking peppermints
enthusiastically.
Slamming doors resound around cars parked.

On the air is the smell of sweet vomit
as it splashes on the tarmac.
A parent yells,
and a boy falls in to her car.

We leave for home and the girls speak in code.
2.4.1, successfully ordered on false ID.
Someone is in tears,
Always the same.

No drugs on them,
Not tonight anyway.
King Alfred, is keeping watch.

---

36. **King Alfred's Statue: Twyford Down Road Protest** *Trish*

They'd gather here to march,
beneath King Alfred's stern gaze

An army of sorts,
not saving us from Viking threat
this time, but rather, saving us from ourselves
from our love affair with motor cars

Some protesters come from Winchester
some come from far away
some come on foot
some come by bike
some come to play reggae
on a small sound system

Once Keats declared the air on Twyford Down
worth six pence a pint;

not any more. Keats knew not
of infernal combustion
nor of the A34

Down the High Street they march,
a ragged reconstruction of a mediaeval past
but the standard-bearers bear no coats of arms,
just Earth First, Profits Last.
These are people taking a stand for their land
walking tall for the good of all,
a warrior band noble in outlook
and unconventional in equipment:

some have bongos
some have djembe drums
one has a love heart
in paint on her tum
one has a didgeridoo
one has antlers on his head
and one has come
in some sort of pink tutu
with morris bells attached.

*Now head west, up the High Street. All the
following moments – the rest of this walk – occur
along this long and ancient strip of wonder.*

Broadway & Lower High St

Bottom of High Street Haiku

---

37. **Bus Station Haiku** *Miriam Jeffrey*

It's sad. She's going.
Seems just so quick. The bus leaves
in 10. What's to say?

---

38. **Bench, front of Guildhall** *Anastasia, age 6*

Don't ride my skateboard;
I just sit and roll on it,
but it still moves me.

---

39. **The Broadway** *MCS*

Farmers' Market Day
Is that the price of chicken!?
I go to Tesco.

40. **Winchester Hat Fair**   *A Crowdsourced Poem*

It's like a rainbow crash landing on the streets
It's librarians up ladders
and you get to meet a ten-foot talking camel
It's your ribs getting tickled and
     your mind blown
It's completely bonkers
It's the kickstart on the motorbike of summer
It's make-up and it's stilts
it's doing-what-thou-wilt

It's packed pavements
It's a lack of cars
It's unicycle jugglers and queuing at bars
It's the only thing stopping Winchester
disappearing up its arse
It's brilliant fun
It's ace
It's not to Nigel's taste (Nigel is my brother)
It's this city's heart
It's a hat full of soul
I'd prefer less juggling,
but on the whole,
I enjoy it.

41. **Hat Fair, High Street** *Clare B*

Antarctic Explorers dragging
their sleds of supplies
up the High Street in July;

toddlers following
like penguins,

the coldest faces
melting into smiles.

42. **Chococo Chocoku** *MCS*

Buying my father
a great treat in chocolate
Mini King Alfreds.

43. **Flat Above The Halifax**   *Stephen*

One flat above the Halifax
One flat roof

One concept
One script
One toy gun
One camera

One pair of twitching curtains
One neighbour who jumps
to conclusions.

One locked down street,
Ten armed cops smashing at the door.

44. **Middle Brook Street Haiku**   *MCS*

Midnight at new year
we dance, laughing, down the street.
Our daughter cringes.

45. **Sainsbury's, Middle Brook St**
Ellie, Kim & Unknown

We just moved in. We all just met.
We're strangers to this city,
to each other, too, but together
we've a Uni flat, an empty kitchen
needing bread and milk, a range of
soothing herbal teas.

Who knows how soon we'll have to
hold each other's hands? Laugh or weep,

feel the need to stick the kettle on.
So here we are. All for one and one for all.

To each of us an orange plastic Sainsbury's bag
and stuffed with bog roll,
    HobNobs and ibuprofen.
Our coded badge. Our gang tattoo. Our
    new allegiance,
sworn in perishable goods.

46. **Poundland** *Penny Monro*

A cotton bud flattened in the gutter
near a drain, beside the bus station,
discarded, nose discoloured, bent
as the old woman stepping from
the country bus, her brown coat, a shell
clasping her lolling bag.

Tottering, slow, flattened feet,
she counts the chewing gum gobs,
measled pavements, to Poundland
opposite discontinued designer,
the cheap chocolate, soap, face powder,
clasping her lolling bag.

Easy to slip pristine cotton buds
un-soiled, peppermint gum, a
chocolate bar, ginger nuts, that
hot water bottle, a Christmas
fairy for new lonely company,
into her empty lolling bag.

47. **Baker's Arms, High Street** *Angela*

We loved it there;
Down the alley,
the smokey back rooms
the outside seats.

Underneath the glass verandah,
with drink after laughing drink
til the roof support proved
too hard to resist

and we pole-danced
our way to ankle-sprains
and hangovers.

48. **Baker's Arms Haiku** *Malcolm*

This is where we met.
Legs, smile and a blue striped dress.

That smile still does it.

49. **Inside Tesco Metro Haiku**   *Alison*

By the frozen fish
Joe (five), denied a Twix, screams.
Swallow me now, earth.

50. **Outside Tesco Metro Haiku**   *Penny Monro*

Big Issue banter
scarfed woman's sallow skin
patience each day

51. **Outside White's, The Pentice**   *Helen*

My brother, over from New Zealand,
stops just here. Demands to know, *if we're*
a city, right, then how come almost every
other person on the street seems to know you?
So many stop and smile and greet me by my
name.

Node Point #4: Buttercross

Buttercross Haiku

---

52. **Summer, Late Eighties** *Ste*

We spent summer here.
My first cider. Merrydown.
Bill played Clash tapes loud.

---

53. **We Were All Goths Then** *Ellie Bignall*

We wasted hours there.
Bunked off school to sit and pose
Crimped hair and roll-ups.

---

54. **After the Gig** *Mel U.*

Stone made your bum ache.
Su was sick through her fingers;
satan's waterfall.

55. **Buttercross** *Anon*

A busker is playing the guitar
on the steps of the Buttercross
when, from out of the crowd
a dancer suddenly joins.

It is a spontaneous moment,
and the increase in applause
and the increase in coins
has us understand
the act of unplanned humanity
has increased our enjoyment
more than double;
the employment of feet
is well worth the trouble.

I love a union of workers
I love a union of love
I love a union of arts

This guitarist is now greater
than the strumming

of his parts.

56. **Frank** *Emma Sumpster*

He believed in living lightly.

Squirrelled away in his bender,
a homemade tent of woven poles
and patched tarpaulin, stuffed
with books.

Frank didn't want for much, it seemed.
Just knowledge, a few good stories
and a bit of food for his dogs.

You'd watch them all,
traipsing to the Buttercross
to busk, his smiley face
the colour and texture
of old leather.

Of course, he couldn't
be allowed to stay.

He believed in living lightly.

It made it easy for them to clear
every trace of him away.

57. **Buttercross: Safety Last!**   *Penny Monro*

A one-eyed clock, hung time,
like Harold Lloyd, clinging
from a metal hand, black
as all the beams of Boots

across the bustled street
opposite a single legless
swinging boot high above
the tip tapping of

double heels, the rubber suck
of trainers, the slurp of wellies,
each twenty-four I ratchet
round, evading pigeons who

escape roofed chicken wire
scrunched, coiled, their prison
before being drenched or
drowned in gutter sludge

and beneath the Buttercross's
frost fractured finial there's busking
as the frazzled two-leggers
crowd the Styx – a choice:

Beyond kingly helmet, up wooded
hill to heavenly cowslips, butterfly
reserve? Or, a nearer inferno
of flambé greed, exterior flames?

Harold Lloyd reference:
'Safety Last!' – 1923 Criterion Collection film

The Omphalos of the City

Omphalos */ˈɒmfələʊs/ noun*

1. (Literary) the centre or hub of something.

"this was the omphalos of confusion"

2. (in ancient Greece) a conical stone (especially that at Delphi) representing the navel of the earth.

And this brings us to the conclusion of this walk. The Omphalos of Winchester, the ultimate node point, the main residence of the Genius Loci, the bijou pied-a-terre of the Spirit of Place.

This is the one spot – and an unlikely one at that – that came up more than any other across the city in the memories and moments of Winchester's citizens. Of course, the cathedral and its environs have already showed themselves to be the focus of a wide spectrum of activity, both godly and less so, but these 'holy grounds' cover a fairly expansive area. This spot, on the other hand, occupies only a few litter-strewn square metres, at the 'dull end' of the High Street, away from the hubbub of the main shopping centre and the bustle of the cathedral approaches.

'Horse and Rider', a pretty-much-life-size 1974 bronze sculpture by Dame Elizabeth Frink, is one of those pieces of inoffensive public art that local authorities love to provide, presumably for the 'betterment' of their citizens. One assumes that whoever signed off the purchase order had visions of Winchester residents and tourists stopping to nod, point, admire and, perhaps, move on to a reasonably-priced eaterie to further discuss notions of art and aesthetics.

But, in a triumphant display of the refusal of the human spirit to go along with municipal ideas of the public good, the people of Winchester have – as the following poems serve to illustrate – instead chosen to employ the statue as a venue for a broader range of activities, including drunkenness, debasement, showing off, singing, parkour, vomiting, urination, necking, fornication, serious injury and senseless violence. The only category from my Unforgettable Moments map that wasn't repeatedly fulfilled was 'Supernatural'. If there *is* a ghost here, people have been having (generally) far too good a time to notice.

Node Point #5:
Omphalos (Supreme Node):
Horse & Rider Statue,
Upper High Street

58. **Horse & Rider: Violent Interlude**

When I said
Mate, are you starting?
I meant it as an honest question;
I find it hard to read the signs.

He took it as a first punch swung,
came in with his fists and feet,
and mates behind him, bent on harm;

my mate, trying to appeal for calm,
got exactly nowhere. Well, in truth,
got knocked back into the bush,

got scratched to fuck. I lost a tooth.
And then they disappeared. And left
just us, the roar of midnight cars,

and that horse, who just looked the other way.

Horse & Ri-ku

---

59. **New Year's Eve** *Jacob*

Threw the night back up,
I did. Behind the horse, while
my sweet girlfriend laughed.

---

60. **Stephanie** *Martin*

We met here Fridays,
after work. Her knitted hat,
yellow autumn leaves.

---

61. **Prelude to a Hangover** *Stevie W.*

A bottle of wine
drunk sat behind the rider
my last memory

62. **Horse & Rider: Untitled**

Liz, Mick and anon.

It's a natural stopping point,
staggering uphill to home;
the place you'd break to snog,
to piss, to wait for them to
catch you up. The horse
just doesn't care, the rider, too;
let the people do what people must.
We'd just wish the bloody thing
could move, could carry us
to bed, like in some fairy tale
where the protagonists are
amiable drunks instead of kids.

---

63. **Horse and Rider**   *Many and various*

Julie says she's often sat astride,
dead of night, the silver spotlight
of the summer moon glinting off
the Pinot Noir clutched, half-empty, in
her unsteady hand as the lads serenade
her with lager-whipped whoops and cheers,
and Billy tried to stand straight up,
which landed him in A&E, slurring apologies

to all his mocking mates for having them
miss the Libertines gig
Trev *did* stand up – so he says; in fact, sang
all of *Common People* at the passing knots
of art-school kids, back in '98
when doing that could still impress;
Rosie tore her graduation dress
and nearly sprained an ankle
and Frank and Joe, Martin, Gary
Jane and even smiley Mylene,
all have nipped behind the steed
to snatch a crafty piss.

And this is the irony –
the rider's blessed
with the sort of face that compels
a certain sort of bloke to offer up
a cheer up mate, it might never happen,
when of course it always happens.
It happened then. It happens now.
Day in, day out. It happens time
and time and time again –
students climbing on his shoulders
Subways bag shoved in his hand
Saints scarves and traffic cones
and bird shit dripping down his nipples.

Going nowhere, yet still somehow
such a part of so many journeys;
Horse & Rider, heads slightly turned,
to gaze in hope straight up the street –
as if that hope, and hope alone,
can resurrect Alfred's purging armies
or summon forth a van of saviour coppers.

---

64. Horse & Rider   *Ash*

Here on a whim,
writing poetry on a wall
next to the Horse & Rider,
trying to think what moment
I should write

But picking on one is like
trying to focus on one ray of light
in a running river.

So I think I'll pick this moment.
This present is enough.

OUTLIERS

Other moments / poems from the 'outer' city centre

65. **Jewry Street: Theatre Royal**   *Sue Spiers*

Six of us wait to be let in.
Jean is expected, but late.
The duty manager opens
the stage door and we file in.
We climb steep, green stairs,
three flights of non-slip lino,
ugly and reminiscent of moss.
I stop at each landing
to catch my breath, thankful
this only happens monthly.
Alex has the key to a door
at the top, level with the Gods,
to a room where actors dress,
the clothes rails at the far side
dangle a single coat hanger.
Geoff finds the ventilation
button and air-conditioning
chills the stuffy room.
We unfold trestle tables,
unpack pads, papers, agenda,
water bottles, throat sweets.
When Jean arrives, with crutch,
the knee operation's discussed.
We settle ourselves to begin.

The ladies exclaim "O"
like Supremes in close harmony
as wardrobe doors crash open
and spill a naked couple.

---

66. Theatre Royal   *Brenda*

My daughter, she started here.
Got picked up as a model; then
came *Eyes Wide Shut,* starred alongside
Kidman, Cruise. Got deeper into film,
then dumped it all. The Weinstein
culture was too much to bear;
eyes wide shut no longer.

67. **Discovery Centre: Winchester Poetry Festival** *Catherine*

As a nurse, I feel
like an imposter
at a poetry festival;
just for this moment,
I've joined another world.

68. **Hyde St: The Mucky Duck** *Anna*

We are watching the opening ceremony
of the London Olympics on the big screen

and we are surprised to find
our eyes are full of tears

and our hearts are full of pride
and we are laughing because

we are not sure why.

69. **Hyde Church Lane:**
   Winchester Lido Ballroom   *David H*

The bands used to play on wooden boxes
on top of the pump room machinery

It was the biggest space in town.
In through the lido side door,
all the gang would be there –
Paul Tubbs, Perky Hayes –
come for Acker Bilk, The Stones
The Kinks, and all the other greats.

They'd come for them, and trouble, too;
in the lane that ran outside
Perky gave the deathray glare
to Keef out the Rolling Stones;
the lads had to hold him back, and

once, I danced with Perky's wife,
and that was that. Got me marked.
Couldn't go back there again, so
sorry, mate, I can't give you other stories.

Christ knows what he did to her.

70. **Hyde Church Lane:** **Winchester Lido, July 1968**   *Sally Russell*

I queue in savage sun
at the green gate, rolled towel
and cozzy under my arm.

    I love to live so pleasantly

Melted, we're admitted
after half-past two, heat-softened
flip flops bendy on my feet.

    Live this life of luxury

Squeezed my towel between
crisping teenagers – Barbie-pink tranny
tuned to Fluff's Pick of the Pops.

    Lazin' on a sunny afternoon

Bodies toast on the terrace.
My white-pink skin, flushed
with an overdose of UVB.

    In the summertime

Wafts of Coppertone and chlorine
remind me of the ice-cream stand
at Bournemouth beach.

    In the summertime

Soles of my feet fry on hot stone.
I slip into the shallow end—toes sizzle
like spit on a griddle.

In the summertime

Dripping wet, I line up
at the hole-in-the-wall with 1/6
for a Bovril and a wagon wheel.

(Lyrics from 'Sunny Afternoon' by Ray Davies)

---

71. North Walls Park, humpback bridge: My Mother Loved Herons   *Anon*

So, sat there, by the river
on her birthday, I'm
thinking of her and a
heron lands, out of
the June blue
and stands,
as close to me
as you are.

And I just knew.
I *knew*.

72. **University, Romsey Rd: Epiphany**   *Emma*

Getting bawled out
for a late essay
a couple of days
after coming out
of hospital
decided me;

who wants to be
an RE teacher anyway?

They say
god moves
in mysterious ways;
that day
she held open
the door and
poured sunshine
on the pavement outside,
too inviting to ignore.

73. **No. 9 (exact location redacted)**
Anthony Cavender

As soon as we walked round the corner, and
Down the communal drive,
We knew –
This is the place!
The day was crisp and bright with promise,
Spring unfurling in leaves and buds and
blossom.
The right time for a new start.
The sun warmed redbrick walls, made white
shutters blaze.
A green door opened to welcome us in.

PART II: PEOPLE, PLACES & PROJECTS

Poems commissioned to celebrate city-centre personalities, businesses and social projects that help to shape the identity of Winchester. There are so many more people worth celebrating. Choose one yourself, and immortalise them in words.

Bespoke Biking: All for Bikes, Not for Profit

There are few things as beautiful
as a bicycle.

Think about it. The Bicycle.

What other mode of transport
does you the more good
the more you use it?

A bicycle is a pinnacle
of human invention
it amplifies your power
it empowers your feet

A bicycle lends wings to the poor

it dispels the traffic
it frees up the air
it's cheap and enriching
and friendly, so there
are no reasons not to get
a bike.

There are few things as beautiful
as social enterprise.
Think about it. Social enterprise.

People putting their arms
around their community

for the common good
for the enrichment of humans;
surely this is how the world *should* run?

Hands reaching down
to help each other up
Uplifting. Upskilling
Unleashing the thrilling
feeling of building something together
watching human seeds become trees;
small cogs becoming freewheeling bikes

There are few things as beautiful
as Bespoke Biking

All for Bikes
Not for profit
What not to be liking?

It's a Team:
for all at Bespoke & Handlebar Cafe

There's Jim and Phil
who sort out the training
and Lee with the steady hand
There's Hannah with spanners
And Joe on the hiring and
the rest of the workshop band

There's Doris and Lily whose
coffees are perfect, whose bacon
is done to a T. And so many more
who work to ensure your
breakfast's the best it could be

So you see

it's glorious and giving
and people-enriching;

it's a wheel with many spokes
and the turn of each day
is a revolution.

Bespoke Biking: A Poem for Heather

Heather has a heartbeat
that sounds like the steady
tick of a freewheel

Heather has a soul
like a magnet
for good coffee
and braised downtubes
and humans needing direction

Heather has hands
that like to do good,

that cannot strip down
a disc brake or straighten a wheel
or cook up the fried sausage sarnies
but that can draw in the people
who can.

Heather has a bicycle
that sticks to back lanes
carries shopping in panniers
has a gutload of kindness
tied to its rack

Heather has a gift
for finding the best path
for finding the best in people
for inviting humanity into the saddle
and giving it a backie
all the way home.

Projects Kitchen & Store: A Poem for Cassie

They come to interview her in the Maldives, the copy
half-written in their heads, their speedboats bouncing

off the cobalt waves toward her island. After all, her
story's so well-known – first Winchester, then Frome,

then this is where it leads, this is what the seed
grows into. Their pieces always start '*she was always one to*

do her thing', '*She was no good at taking direction*'. When they ask her secret at the end,
she'll always say

it's the way she manages people; she'll big up
that she sees them all as mates, and you look
out for your mates.

People know that they can count on you. She's
proud, she says, as she sips vodka from a cowrie
shell, proud

that no-one's quit and not still remained a
friend. *Projects*

was always more than just a caff, a shop, she'll say. It was

always more about community. All those strange and lovely folk, who had their stalls, who popped in and out to get

their cut. And, of course, the cafe crew; we were a gang together. Charlotte, Becky, Big Daddy Craig and the rest,

Good guys, one and all, we only had the best. And they'll ask if she misses Winchester, and she'll concede the city

etched itself somehow on her soul. After all, it was the start. And Boomtown still burns bright in her youthful heart. And

when the press guys take their leave, climb back into their boats and head for where the wifi is, she'll sum it up, treat

them to her key to life, and this is it:

be nice to people, and don't take any shit.

Piecaramba! A Poem for Rob & the team

If life is one great massive pie –and it is –
then you have to be true to your filling.
You have to be willing to peel back your crust
and trust your own authentic recipe
if you can just learn to savour your flavour
then you will be favoured on the lips
    of the masses.

So, take one small building.
Add a sprinkle of community,
a dash of friendship,
a love of independent spirit
a desire to do something different
Top it off with a soupcon of stilton
and a tasty pastry of pop culture.

The kids love it
The dads go mad for it
From Pokemon to Walking Dead
From Vampire Slayers to Stranger Things
Create a place where food tastes ace
the staff laugh, Nintendos ping
beneath the gaze of cartoon zombie hordes.
It will be a smash.

One man's dream gone pie-shaped
and served with liquor and mash.

Donna Laine Jewellers: A Poem for Donna

As a child she fell in love
with a blue spark in the snow
at a Birmingham bus stop;
a sapphire unstuck. A holy glow
and she had the luck to catch its eye

As a child she fell in love
with a spark in the snow;
and every jeweller knows
a stone can speak to you
a stone can wink at you
a stone can come alive
a stone can fall in love back

She fell in love
with a spark in the snow
and wouldn't you know?
the spark became a flame
and now her name's on the front
of a shop; a gem set in the crown
of a city as tight as a village
and warm as gold

She can show you a rainbow
in the blink of a diamond.
She can polish old pearls
so they look alive.
She cuts so fine.
She shuts at five.
She gives the shine
back to granny's necklace.
She can take the old off rose gold
to leave it rose golder
She can hang from your earlobes
or between your shoulders
She can do great things

She can make rings
that sing the words
of every brilliant love song
in your voice.

P&G Wells Bookshop: A Poem for Steve

Behold this paragon of man,
who bears the weight of history
on only-slightly-complaining shoulders;

a man so absorbed in beautiful duty
his own internal organs have rearranged
alphabetically on ribcage shelves,
whose blood cells are order forms for oxygen,
whose heartbeat is an echo on a box-strewn
stairwell.

Look at him; his legs toned by
a thousand miles of bicycle deliveries,
his spectacles the windows
of an Emporium of Human Enrichment.

It was he who sanded back these ancient
floorboards
to find, written in the swirling grain, his
destiny:

Knowledge-shepherd.
Enabler for creative urges.
Travel agent for the imagination.

P & G Wells Bookshop

Think how many flannelled oiks
have popped in here for pens and ink,
and gone to school, and finished school
and hit the world and made their mark
and then grown old and fat and died.

And think of all the folk who've
picked a book, and bought a book
and tripped up on a turn of phrase
and tumbled heartlong into love.

And think how it was horses once, and dirt
for streets, and now it's cars and vans
and people staring at their phones
and all the while, through all of it,
as generation after generation has
been born, has blossomed, bloomed
and withered, has nudged the sum
of all we've done a further inch or two
along the path, all this while
this place has stood, right here,
doing just what it was born to do.
We're used to stuff that doesn't last;
no sooner out the box than in the bin,
pubs and shops and even streets

seem duty bound to change their names
or change their shapes or let themselves
get swept out of existence.

But not this place. Think of all the
tortured nights, the tears, the pacing
and the writer's blocks required
to fill two hundred years of shelves
with the cream of brains and souls.

It's like a museum to artistic pain and glory,
it's like an ancient sleepy beast whose dusty
eyes have witnessed the evolution of the punter –
from wigs and frocks, through stovepipe hats,
to bowlers, boaters, then no hats at all,

as the city round it ebbs and flows,
as philosophies and fashions come and go,

it's just sat here, like some great
Galapagos turtle, stuffed with words.

Gervades Dry Cleaning

Special moments start here
in a shop the size of a postage stamp
with an ironing board like a dining table
and a sewing machine cowering beneath
a giant photo-print of the Cathedral.

Special moments start with Ewa, the Polish
seamstress, who sits at that battered Singer,
and with Steve, bagging up the clean stuff,
a tattooed Saints badge rippling on his calf

and of course special moments
    start with Javaid,
working the floor like a dapper Tigger, spinning
off-the-cuff philosophy behind a Covid mask
that spills, from out its sides, smiles warm
as duvets spilling out from plastic wrappers.

Special moments start here –
with these three friends,
working under bright strip lights
like someone flattened the sun
in the trouser press,

surrounded by giant photographs,
printers buried under sheets
and cameras piled on invoice pads.

It's not an everyday place, and
it's not a place for everyday;
these three have no interest
in your pants and socks

Special moments start here –
this is interviews and marriages,
this is funerals and graduations;
this is first dates and birthdays
with a zero at the end

This is for when
the phone call comes, the email
pings; the days the world grows
or shows its love or sheds a tear

This is for when the city knows
it simply has to look its best.

Stardust Years Vintage: A Poem for Karen

Look at her. Sits in here, behind the counter,
    waiting on
the dial phone to ring, to offer her a part;
    a stage role

cast in Bakelite and sure, she'll have
    something good to
wear, no doubt, straight off her racks, a
    nd lipstick every

shade of midnight waiting room to boot. Above
the city, potty-mouthed microwaves are
bouncing off cathedral

walls, pinging dick-pics and discount codes to a
populace more attuned to tiny screens, and
even grannies here are

wearing day-glo trainers. This is not a world for
her; she lights candles on the Bette Davis
shrine, cuddles lop-eared

bunnies in a quiet corner, and barricades
    the door. She'll
be alright, she thinks; she's holed up with
    a good supply

of Rayne heels and dresses of the sort of cut
that get asked out by calling cards, not one-line
texts, and she's wrapped

herself against this all-pervading dark with a
stardust coat sewn from half-remembered
closing lines and memories

of ice-cream trays hung from swan-necked
girls. So when that phone rings, she'll be ready.
She's written the card;

she'll put it in the window as she goes.
    Just popped out
    to 1937.
    Back in two twitches of a rabbit's nose.

The Community Pantry / Winchester Mutual Aid

It's about sitting down
with the world, pulling up
a chair and sharing a cuppa

It's about people being seen,
people being heard. It's
about people rolling the word
dignity around their tongues
for the first time in however
long, savouring the flavour,
enjoying choices in lives
that don't see many.

It's about letting people know
that they are OK, that they
are more than the hands dealt
them from a weighted deck.

So come on in, my friends –
browse these tables, take
what you like. Right here,
there's enough in the world
to go round. Try something new.
Feel your chains get lighter.

You are worth it.

A Poem for Diane Grudgings, City Tour Guide

Stuffed in the pockets of her black coat are
dates and words
and all the stuff you need to build
    the story of a city, and
everywhere she goes, she drops a
    weird litter of facts.

She knows the bishop's dirty shame,
has loads of ghosts for mates
and forgotten people use her mouth to talk.

By the Westgate she'll stand, looking down the
High Street's length into the eyes of Romans,
and when she walks, she'll dodge in and out of
gates and walls our

simple minds don't know enough to see.
    The past
is a hypnotic tune, and when she plays she has
them all transfixed – the tourists, kids, the
passers-by, all begging

for the hows and whys and whens, keen for
gore, for riots, routs and poor Fanny Adams. A
pied piper leading us away from our tired world
of traffic jams and bags for life,

we let her paint her pictures in our heads,
    do weird things
to all our clocks and reanimate the dead.
Stephen and Mathilda, old deBlois, and William
Ogle, too drunk to get up on his horse; her
knowledge the defibrillator that gets the blood
back coursing through their veins, and into
ours.

The Eclipse Inn: Lady Alice's Ghost

She's been in here full 300 years, sits
in the corner, minds her own business,
sometimes seen, more often not. Her
grey frock has not one stain from spilled
beer, no ash-smudges from drunken fags,
the mores the pity, she thinks; half the people
come in here because of her, but no-one
seems to see it fit to buy her a bloody drink.

And god, she thinks, it's all so *quiet* now –
not just the lack of hammered shouts as the
cruel shape of her last stand emerges
in the square outside, but quiet full stop,

and Terri, who's in charge downstairs,
she'd be the first to echo that. *She* came
here from Eastleigh 'Spoons: steering
drunks toward the door, stopping fights
and mopping up the vomit. Here, there's
none of that, just a lot of tourist trade,
drawn in by the history, by *her*story;
come to see the little pub where they
killed a woman, just because they could.

And that killed woman watches them;
across the heaving bar of time, she sees them

ordering their lunches and their useless halves,
flicking through their city maps.

The irony, of course, in life, you'd never catch
her dead in drinking holes of any sort. But now,
she hankers for the company of drunks; craves
the lost, the lonely, all those drowning busted
hearts – pissed and wailing in the snugs.

She can't annihilate the horror
    that was done her,
see; can't drink away the past. Instead,
    she finds
kinship in the shared pain. In watching others
lose their head.

Warrens Stationers

You want pens? We've got pens.
Pens for every conceivable need.
Pens to write, to scribble, to draw.
Pens so ergonomically gorgeous
they make your heart bleed ink

You want paper? We've got paper.
All the sizes, all the weights.
All the different tonal shades
and some great day-glo sheets
if discrete is not your thing

And staples. Don't talk to us about *staples*.
Actually, *do* talk to us about staples;
you will find no human anywhere
that knows as much, or loves, or cares
about the minutiae of stationery as us.

We are Warrens. We are a team.
Twined as tight as paperclips;
stuck together like Pritt. Chris
and Sam and Gill and Nath and
Sophie, too; here since 1835,
and written through our very hearts
are the words Customer Service
in a range of permanent colours.

Winchester BID

We are the icing on the cake
We are the crown on the king
We are the sparkle and the bling
We are the environment enhancer

We are like the bells on the trousers
of a morris dancer
called Winchester.

We connect you together.
We work for your good
We big up your 'hood
We put your oar in the pond
of municipal decisions
We look after your dreams
and protect your visions

We're shaping a city we'd want to live in
We're shaping a city we'd love to see
We're shaping a city we'd want to visit
We're shaping a city and it can be
a very many-splendoured thing –

we organise the hanging baskets
we set the gingerbread trails
we put up all the Christmas lights;

being the wind in the sails
of small-scale independents
and big scale independence
is a lot of work

But the Joy in a hand-stamped paper bag
The Perfection in a steaming cup
The Satisfaction in the smile of a City Ranger
The lifting of a city up
makes all of it so worth it.

Winchester Magazine and Liz Kavanagh

Point of Light

We are an army, scrambled at the click of a
mouse
and armed to the teeth with kindness.
When the hospital needs radios,
then they shall have radios
When they cry out for fridges
then they shall have fridges
When there's a need for ten thousand baubles
to brighten the wards
then supply lines are activated,
a thousand hearts pump love to our hands
and our hands bring hope to the people.
Together we can do great things;
we can get snacks for nurses,
bring doughnuts to bus drivers
we can be the arms around you,
holding you up in these troubled times.

We are an army.
We are community.
We march to a drumbeat named *In It Together*.
We fight on a diet of well-written words.
Our badge reads Who Cares, Wins.